WUNDERKAMMER

Also by Cynthia Cruz

Ruin
The Glimmering Room

WUNDERKAMMER

Cynthia Cruz

Four Way Books
Tribeca

Please direct all inquiries to:
Editorial Office
Four Way Books
POB 535, Village Station
New York, NY 10014
www.fourwaybooks.com

Library of Congress Cataloging-in-Publication Data

Cruz, Cynthia.
[Poems. Selections]
Wunderkammer / Cynthia Cruz.
pages cm
ISBN 978-1-935536-47-5 (pbk. : alk. paper)
I. Title.
PS3603.R893A6 2014
811'.6--dc23
2014011289

This book is manufactured in the United States of America and printed on acid-free paper.

Four Way Books is a not-for-profit literary press. We are grateful for the assistance
we receive from individual donors, public arts agencies, and private foundations.

This publication is made possible with public funds from the National Endowment for the Arts

NYSCA

and from the New York State Council on the Arts, a state agency.

[clmp]

We are a proud member of the Council of Literary Magazines and Presses.

Distributed by University Press of New England
One Court Street, Lebanon, NH 03766

TABLE OF CONTENTS

THREE

NEBENWELT

Subverted my psychosis to watery ornament.
Was found drowned in a cream velvet
Mini gown, mind blown out like a city
With no electricity, all lines cut.
The brain, a kaleidoscopic disco.
But nothing another viewing of *Mother
Courage* couldn't fix. And a trunk labeled
Trauma packed with piles of miniature Steiff.
I was dreaming evacuation.
Watching at the locked glass window, I can see
The satanic mills of industry. And the small white
Horse dragging the carriage of lost memory.
Rapturous, an accordion plays God
Save the Queen and Paris is Burning.
After I licked clean the saucers
Of Schlag and ceiling-high cream cakes,
I ran twelve miles in my ballet leotard
Through the German forest of snow.
How do I feel about my botched suicide?
Lacing up my skating boots, I
Vanish, silvery paste of vapor on the ice.
A row of pretty blonde dummies in the Dutch death
Museum, death dressed in Chanel and Maharaja
Paste jewels, a vibrant green bacteria of sea and decay.

ONE

WUNDERKAMMER

A Greek crime mars the pastoral.
Charts and maps, an atlas of anesthesia-
Laced nostalgia. A long haired, white
Rabbit, muffled, shot, and stuffed.
An old yellow chiffon gown, the ribbon
Hem, ripped and red wine stained.
Curricula of the mundane.
Symptoms of trauma, like ghost
Spots of water on crystal
That will not be washed off.

WONDER ROOM

Welcome to the dawn of the haunted.

Kingdom of what, or whether,
Or not, I wanted it.

The machine that measures beauty.
The machine

Is feeding into me.
An IV drip of consumption, whether or not

I want it. Fashion and excess.
Decadence, and its magnificent diamond

Of glut,
Glittering its warm doom and contagion.

Eleven years of ballet
Cannot stop me

From starving.
The incessant rush

Of memory, the glut.
I swear

The earth is still humming.

SELF PORTRAIT IN AIRPORT CITY

Pharmacopoia blonde in yellow
Fogal stockings, She Uemera
Royal crimson nail polish, and
Glam cream shadow
In pearl matte. Gold taffeta
Disaster blouse. My long dirty
Blonde hair, pulled back
In a jewel-embellished French
Barrette and bits of shredded
Paper ribbons. Sea-weed like
Debris of what's left.

THE INVISIBLE KINGDOM

Over the Orinoco
Through the black fields
Of what once was Eden.

A queen in a glass
Palanquin,
I slept through the burning

And was laid flat on the grass
Like a child
Dragged in from the ocean.

In the morning, three singing women arrived.
They slit open the lung of my belly.
But there were no babies inside,

Just green sea foam and jewel-
Encrusted earthworms.
These words, this terrible song.

NEBENWELT

When I was seven death
Crept into me: black shellacked
And lavatorial, it dragged me
Down to its sea of drowned
Animals, their wet fur, elaborate
Blankets clinging to their bodies,
Their eyes, Swarovski glittering
In the brine of the green ocean.
I nearly went blind, then,
As it lead me further.
Down, it drove me to the baby:
Spoon-fed, and senseless. Like music
For centuries. I swam in its murk and
Viscera, its worrying warm milk
Whispering to me. Elysian,
Wandering the dark fields,
Its cathedrals of speech, and its shut
Doors. Until the world was a room
Of silver mollusks and eels, old black and white
Photographs, and obsolete maps strung on the walls.
I lost my voice. Then the delicate
Metal clasp came undone. Mother,
I never recovered. Childlike
Inside my middle-aged body I am
Sleepwalking inside the whirring
Factory of my memory-less life, I am

Waiting, impatiently, for the violent
White song of the ambulance
Siren when it comes to take me,
Finally wake me.

SELF PORTRAIT IN EMERALDS, WITH MUSIC

Sitting cross-legged inside a wide circle of pills,
In my childhood costume of pale pink
Leotard, chalk white stockings
And black Balenciaga three-inch heels.
Face made miraculously matte
With Chanel cream paste makeup,
And cat-whiskers painted on my face
In liquid liner from another night
I can't remember.

MNEMOSYNE ATLAS

Out of nowhere, a drown of music,
Probably dead or else, Bohemian.

What gorgeous, and out of nowhere.
And glittering. A silver waste, a warm

Unknown paste of pearl
And jewels. Some small foods.

It's true. I lose
My mind, but I get

This, instead. What appears,
Warm, like a dream

This train, and humming,
Windows of glass emerald.

When the singing begins,
I step over the silver

Wheels, and drop down
Into the music,

A secret entering the body.
Or summer, southern, at dusk.

Blackstrap molasses, slow
Thick, a ticking

In the velvet.
An internal mars,

A sweet swamp, electric,
A flicker at first, then lost.

Blinding and blue
This God-like narcotic—

NACHLEBEN

In the dream factory, Angel carries the ward
Boombox on his one good shoulder, shuffling
To his secret beat of nothing. As the East River
And its trash-carrying barges move Risperdon-
Slow past the huge glass windows.
The girls cry at the tables,
Push their food away.
Rheinhard, the German chaplain,
Drops off handfuls of black plastic rosaries,
But nobody can save us.
An incessant drone, death
Lives just around the corner, a moon
Moving silently beneath the world,
The sweet bloody hum of the impossible animal.

SELF PORTRAIT WITH THREE MAGI

In my embellishments of lost ballet
And beauty, the three Magi

Come down from the kingdom
In their glittering white crowns

Of Benzedrine. I am their one lost star,
Their flower, drowning.

It takes me hours to form
A full sentence.

They leave on their cream-
and-white dappled horses,

Back into the border
Of the night

Before I can begin.

I waited in a sweet delirium of miracles
To be found out.

And at times, I swear, I could see directly
Into the thing I was

In the forest,
Before the bells finally woke me.

This is my final drag. And I am done

With what the world wanted.

RATTLESNAKES

Meet me with Saint Peter at the all night
AA disco. Halfway to Hades, in the Greyhound
Station bathroom, I cut all my hair off,
Smoked another cigarette until my brain
Finally clicked back on.
God is singing in my head again
In the voice of an insane woman.
What she says I cannot say,
Not to anyone. These days
I parade in mother's long, ice cream–blue gown,
Drinking red wine from a paper cup.
I waited for you on the endless fluorescent
Green lawn of the sanitarium,
Broken diamonds of no sleep.
And I don't remember
A thing. If I could, I would
Love all the boys, weeping.
Administer my poisonous
Heaven to each and every
Beautiful and terrible
One of them.

SLOW DRUG

In the bruise-like blue of the Gloomarium
You sit, nude, at your Bosendorfer
In a Dorotheum of music.
Hides and furs and black tattoos.
Guttural, your ruined, and unfathomable,
Fugue. My love, my darling, my raven-
Haired chaplain, ruminating over your final
Act, your grand masterpiece: Sanatoria
Sonata, Insomnia, Silver Scintilla, the dirty
Hands of Jean Genet. You, my loveliest
Brother, are owned. They won't let you
Go. Not ever. Hotels, salons, and bars:
Nostalgia for what was never. It was
A God-given night when the wind
Howled off the East River, with its
Terrible squalls and brutal endeavors
And we entered the indomitable astonishing.

JUNK GARDEN

Sweet narcosis of blonde
Beers and the recurring image
Of your face.

Annihilating daylight.

Sickly hopeful
In my new black skirt.

Once, when I was a child, I called out your name.

Meanwhile, the exterminating had begun.

An old little girl, I am
Dumb in its blinding.

I move my body
But I never leave this room.

Death row of the soul,
Dirty, train ride.

And I will never

Come back.
This love, trembling—

NEBENWELT

Love, they are taking me now.
Down, to the darker, ward-like stations.
It is German here, in its warp
Of children's murmurs and voices.
For Holiday Pageant, Mother made me
Haloed, angel, wrapped me in iridescence.
Led me to the hay-flocked stage,
My face, pale as a moon,
My grey eyes stare into the white flash
Of her red Sears Roebuck camera.
I am inside my own Berlin,
1985, with its White Duke,
Its zoo, and androgynous. They are following me, calling me names
In German. Like you, I am
Incapable of interpreting my own body,
Its soulless and mollusk iterations.
In the end, I will put a stop to it.
I want to hear the voice speak to me, again.
In a forest, near the border, where Lowell
Went missing after the sanitarium.
On the lake, Bodensee, alone, and with music.

TWO

SELF PORTRAIT WITH COYOTES

Here, in this wilder part of the world, I am
Locked inside a wunderkammer-like
Diorama of hurt music.
Vagabonding in a gunmetal dress
Making my way against the wind
Along the Great Highway.
And the Pacific still smashes
Against cliff rocks, owls
Still live in flocks in oak trees
Before the Exploratorium.
At four I awoke with a vision
Of death, in a hospital bed
In the Excelsior:
Tiger fur, and beaded rings of amethyst
And liquid onyx on fingers.
Crimson ribbons and powder pink
Stockings stitched in sequins.
Everything goes back to the Monroe House,
That strange blasted Eden.
Broken tool, that spilled
Mercury pool.

HOTEL OBLIVION

At Hotel Oblivion, the snow
Goes on for days. A small saga,
Its secret voices bloom against the rotting.
The rooms are painted mint green
Frosting. The men are handsome.
They wear wool blonde suits, take opium,
Ride white horses in a flood
Of bloodhounds, vanishing into the crushed
Black spider of the forest. It hurts
To look at us. Afraid, we mask our faces
In glam makeup to ward off the invisible.
Wear ancient Warhol wigs and Red
Falke or Fogal stockings. We are promiscuous
In our thinness, don't leave the green mansion,
Are trapped inside the snow box, noiselessly
Splendoring. Outside, the bright pines
Weep electric diamonds and stars. At midnight
Supper is served on delicate Dresden
Porcelain: lamb and endless French
Macaroons; Vermouth in small crystal goblets.
When the men return, they let loose
Their horses. Nomadic, they wander
Back defeated to the fortress, broken,
All of this vast collecting, this glamorous
Danger and doom.

ZWISCHENWELT

Queen of Greenpoint, the corner of Ash
And Franklin, in Tante Heidi's hand-me-down

Ermine, high school Levis, boys' size 12.
Queen of autopathology, of dark lit alleys,

Of bars and of vanishing, blonde and vapor.
And emerald green strap heels. My worlds

Are lapping, one flooding over
The other. I am the zoom, the snowball white

Of lithium. Empress of waste and excess. Towers
Of bottles of Triple Sec and Zoo. Chaos,

Herzogian, I am inside my childhood, a no
Man's land of the mind.

Blizzard, a hum, a giddying
Bliss. First aid kits

Of mother's nineteen-seventies makeup:
Grease paint, lipstick, and heaps of nail polish:

Diabolic, Blue Satin, Imperial, and Pink
Mink. Royal icing, a stained script, grammar school

Valentines and old black and white photographs
Strewn through the ten rooms, including the solarium,

Its white mice in silver metal cages, frozen
Inside their tiny landscapes. Before the party,

Mother puts on her face. And Father calls her crazy
Indian. I am on my knees now

Cleaning. The dishes stack in the sink, food goes bad
In the bedroom and the tub changes color.

Reread the Tarot, throw the I Ching. Coat the face
In cold clear jelly

From the cheese box in the fridge.
The doors are always opening

And closing. I'll drive it out of me,
Such majestic horses.

OUT OF THE DESERT HOSPITAL

Awoke in cobalt blue
Fogal stockings, and Kiss
Stage makeup, inside a bathysphere
Of wounding music. A mansion
Of German, rooms of strudel, and quadruple-
Layered raspberry cream cakes.
Starve the shame down to androgyny
And numbness. Beige plastic trays
With my name engraved on them.
A rabbit-eared radio in the cabin is transmitting
The parade of the dead. Dazed, I've lived inside
This adored orphanage, this sorrowful
Wunderkammer. Always gleaning or wasting in its
Accumulating. Darboven panels and a handbook for
Cataloguing the stars. Glam and gloom, a diamond
Gold necklace wrapped around my waist.
In drag, embellishing, collecting, then
Deconstructing to stop the brutal onslaught.

NIGHT LETTERS

At the Hotel Hilton pool
The little girl wades and performs
Saccharine in her bright orange and pink
Swimsuit. Decadence, broken
Stained glass of night, Upstate New York.

I am counting the hours until cocktails
For when I can begin.

And fighting off the high
Priestess of doom, her male
Droves, and their terrible voices.

They are trying to feed me
Their brutal music. I don't want it.
The bleed of memory, the endless
Worry of when I will end. And what
Have I done with this life, anyway.

Like a childhood sickness,
It ticks from the clock
In my head
Where the pulses begin—

Repeating to me what I know already
But do not care
To remember.

SISTER MIDNIGHT

Returned from the underworld,
Its warm blue milk

Streaming
From my shut mouth.

I come from the invisible
Kingdom,

Its scrims of death, its
Forests of flies.

Starving in a delirium,
Ferrying

The wondrous
Blind demons in:

Female, half-crazed, and
In multitudes.

Psychopomp, dragging the flat
Souls of the dead

In through the window
Of this weathered world.

Riding this vessel
Half skiff, half sky

Jet, down into the blacked-
Out spheres of history,

Her tendrils
Of light like sweet

Outreaching,
Chandelier arms.

Night is a sun,
And beneath its false dusk

I'll build an empire.
I will

Live in it, a fevering mutation of broken
Lies.

BATHYSPHERE

Our childhood was a science lab,
A brackish, incubating underworld.
An all-night pharmacy of bright pink
Pills. And the military doctor with his
Throne of medicine, an ossuary of bones.
That dead room of books and sun-bleached
Skulls. No one could protect us. Death
Lurked around the corner, a wild white
Pulse. Incessant drone, sweet hum
Of the animal. Compass with no needle,
We grew old on that waste riddled junk,
With no pilot, no anchor, no map.
Just the warm current of death
Steering us nowhere.

NEBENWELT

Enthralled, I let loose
The brave and beautiful

Lions from their mean, metal
Cages,

Crush the pulse
That raced the ambulance.

Flammable,
The delicate stars

Begin their dimming
One by sour one.

Upon my palm, a bloom
Of bright red

Blood. I destroyed
My body inside

The car crash,
I never had. Spent a lifetime

Inside a box, my mind
A sea of tyranny.

I crawled the long corridor
To the kitchen

Where the windows never stop
Always opening

And closing. Smashed
Ophelia, then floating.

In a glorious red silk kimono,
An army of pin-pearls, and

Diamonds, bulleted
Into its butterfly folds.

Never, Mother says,
And licks shut

The cold black box
Of memory's coffin.

AUTOBIOGRAPHY

Mother was a ballerina, the bruise of her
Limbs hidden in the white cream of grease paint.

When I was eleven, a man took over
My body. And buried me beneath.

Mysterium tremendum, magically
Erased. In Berlin, my mother's mother

Rode her bicycle
To ballet lessons

As the British bombed her city.
Later, soldiers dragged her

Off the street, silenced her
Finally inside a line of burning

Trees. I can't dance.
Some nights, I can't even make

This lame body move.
A crime, and its animals,

The din, I am trying
To tunnel through.

The unburying of the body,
And this terrible singing.

FINAL PERFORMANCE

I crawl along the wet floor
Of my childhood, a serpent,

Or a long-buried secret,
In my mother's bisque

Chiffon gown with small stars
Stitched in silver,

A crown of tinsel
Pinned into the dark

Blonde knots and dreads
Of my hair. I follow a sequin

Thread of dead things,
Get lost in a chaos of glittering,

Stop when the moon clocks out,
Polish my long nails in the sun.

TODESARTEN

I am driving dead
Into it—the wind
Howling against glass
The train racing
Into the mind of the German
Forest.

Whose past am I rattling into? What
Strange limbo of gestation?

I will hide the sealed treasure
Inside the locked hive-
Like box, caging its radiance forever.

I will lick the secret in its shut bonnet.

Someone is coming to me
With a terrible omen,
Moving Biblically,
Centering its danger into me.

I try to move
But the weight is the weight
Of an oil drum
Fixed deep inside me.

Now the oceans have stopped
Their incessant moving.
Four men lift me onto their jewel-
Studded palanquin,

And carry me over the endless
White desert.

When I am lifted out, and laid
Flat on the earth, the animals
Come to me, brushing up against me,
Tasting my palms with their warm wet tongues.

There are no stars in this blue heaven.

If I speak again, it will be
Never.

THREE

NEBENWELT

Quarantined inside a wonderland of endless
Dream: waiting on horseback, at the gate
Of a Dostoyevsky mock death, milky reverie
Of the guillotine. And a room of green and
White coconut cream layered cakes, an infinite
Winter inside them. A childhood of illness.
The moon was the only nurse I knew.
At the shore, I rowed a little rowboat
Out to the end of the world. I found the kill
And entered it. The owl and the pussycat
Rowed in a yellow boat into the gleaming.
Crept out of the playroom
Into the aquarium: Vienna, Salzburg, mildly
German. Mother's cabinets and jewelry boxes.
My small white hands dripping in amethyst,
Pearls, and aquamarine. Woke on the floor,
Slept there, wept there, inside its envelope
Of drowning.

SELF PORTRAIT IN FOX FURS, WITH MAGIC

Where I am the weather is
Spectacular damage, and hustle.

And inside my tiny Berlin,
I am packed, already, in a casket

To be returned in a pearl-
Studded palanquin

With no music. Beneath the blood
And rattle, I saw the moon

Float over a field
Of white horses, a blind king

Whispering in Old German.
They'll hook the gloomed world

Back into me, its menageries
And zoos of wounds, its museums

Of memory, and trauma. In the city
Of palaces, I lived

Inside a doll house
Mansion, Chateau Feral,

Chateau Bloodhound.
Deep inside the primordial forest.

I was born
On its warm floor

Inside the murk of the underworld,
And filled, at birth, with a green ocean of terror.

ATLAS OF THE MOLECULAR KINGDOM OF GIRL ORPHANS

I was carried in a palanquin
By four men
In magnificent costumes.

They wrapped me
In a black dress
As if in a blanket of death.

And left me in a forest
For centuries. When I woke
I was alone

Inside a furnace of bright music.
In the end, I made my way through the never-ending
Atlas of my own making.

SELF PORTRAIT IN DESERT MOTEL ROOM

After the medicine of television, after
Microwave, after the gauze
Is taken off—

A bewildering
Mishap, my long dirty blonde hair
Pulled back—

No beauty in this
Salt-marred diorama of
Silent desperation.

Slide after slide displays
On the wall of the mind:
Goya's black painting

Of Saturn devouring
His own children. Dirt, seed,
Teeth, and the silver

Scintilla, and speed
Of cars flashing past
On their Benzedrine highway.

Glint and warp, accumulation
In the warm blink
Of a locked motel room,

This broke music
Box, of history,
In a gown of glittering

Movement,
Self portrait,
Disguised as human.

THE GAME IS OVER

This is the second underworld
My nurse whispers,
Dragging me down further.

Pretty Harvard hipsters
At the Casablanca.

Bloomingdales and Silver Hills, burning down
Every wing.

Another brother's suicide, another
Cigarette left, lit while sleeping.

Staggering through a lifetime
Of hospitals.

The glass doors swing open.
But where, may I ask

Have they buried
My beautiful children.

PORCELAIN PILLOW IN THE FORM OF A THEATER

The hole in the sky came to me

It whispered to me and I said

No. I won't
Hear it.

But it whispered, with its yellow
Rings and folds of answers.

I lived in dungeons for a century
Wandering up and down the long dank stairs.

And the whispering one
Came again.

And I said, No

I won't speak.

And this time the desert animals came to me
Sat beside me

But they would not love me.

And the sky king came then,
And the moon whirred like a top.

And I walked into the noise and chime of endless procession,
The desert animals falling in folds behind me,

Like an eruption, a terrible forsaken answer,
An endless train of fur and splendor.

KINGDOM OF CLUTTERING SORROW

Another helping of champagne
Cream cake: stacked and beveled,
A miniature cathedral smashed,
Soft white box of sugar and glitter.

Outside, meanwhile, the beige Mercedes
Arrives, its seats of soft red leather.
Its driver, the inventor of sorrow
Takes me across the dead
Zones and bridges
Of America, its eternal labyrinths,
Interlocked, and without meaning.

A collapsible cage
Flocked golden and framed
In wet black lacquer.
And voluminous: dawn's
Museum of stars.

Masked and gowned, I make
My way down
Sokurov's Grand Staircase
Leaving forever behind
The dark kingdom of clutter.

At night the ambassadors arrive
In a ceremony of silent
White blizzard. Carrying goblets and rabbits,
Dragging bags of chain letters.

It's true,
I come from the
Tricked-up hospital
Of beauty and ruin.

I am frozen forever in this wonder
Room, this zoo of one million
Diamond machines.

Come with me into my blonde room
Of music.

Self Portrait as Marilyn
In the Final Sitting.

PASSAGEWAY

Left my bicycle on the edge, then
We made our way

Through the gloom
Of the wet lacquered

Underworld: boarded-up
White stucco hotel

Mansions, poolside canopies,
Tropical entropy. Flotsam

And wealth
In disarray. Nausea,

Miasma, water canisters, and radio
Transistors. And meet me

In the garden.
We could sip some

Sweet, candy-laced
Poison, let the drug of it

Undo us, remove us
To the never

Ending zone of what
The worms left
Of this botched Eden.

HOTEL FERAL

I took the handful of gold capsules
To return my body back
To its center of gravity.

Then dragged myself
To the hotel lobby.

I wanted to find her, that
White rabbit.

I thought I might
Get my mind back.

The answer was glimmering somewhere
In the Porcelain cup

Of oolong tea
Sitting on the long
Black table.

But before I could get there,
The tea, then the answer,
Vanished.

God will place a baby inside me.

By the time you read this
I will be far far away.

Then, I'll come back
With the correct answer.

This is not meant to be a koan
Or a fable.

I am telling you everything.

One day they'll remove
The memory out of me.

SNOWBOUND

When they drag me back
Into this red world with its rabbit
Glue, its skin and wounds,
Its magnificent viscosity, I'll be
Solemn, unscarred, as always,
Countess of innumerable darkness.
A germ, a small poof
Of silence, I move beneath
My imagined furs and stacks
Of beautiful white Warhol wigs.
Madness, perhaps, this schloss.
This wild electric damage
Like Candy Darling alive,
Though barely, on her deathbed.

DEATH SONG

The bloodhounds appeared
On the hillside
Like phantoms

Sniffing up the warm chalk muck
The sun left behind
When the world

Cracked in half.
I didn't sleep
For a century.

And finally woke
When the moon
Arrived: a spool of mew

A dark, death
Lick. I let its sweet
Machinery enter me.

And like a wheel
Of bees, or a live virus,
Destroyed, then nursed back,

I returned to the spore in the center
And like anything
Killed off

I whirred,
A drum, silenced, and kept trapped under
The earth.

SOME VELVET MORNING

Woozy, inside my kremlin of clutter
I drink warm medicinals: Royal
Princess, Everlasting Chiffon
Gown, and Imperial Childhood Tea,
Vanish into the endless
Garden with its brilliant white
Hives of memory, its mausoleums
Of locked, oblong boxes jam-
Packed with history. After the ten year
Junket at the School of Ophelia,
I tried, but finally, could not.
Every time I open my mouth
To speak, just these terrible
Blue diamonds fall out.

ACKNOWLEDGMENTS

Grateful acknowledgment is made to the editors of the following journals in which these poems, sometimes under different titles or in slightly different versions, appeared:

The Academy of American Poets *Poem-a-Day*, *American Poetry Review*, *Anti-*, *Blackbird*, *Boston Review*, *Connotation Press*, *Corresponding Voices*, *The Equalizer*, *Field*, *National Poetry Review*, *Northwest Review*, *Puerto del Sol*, *The San Pedro River Review*, and *Third Coast*.

Cynthia Cruz's poems have been published in *American Poetry Review*, *Boston Review*, *Kenyon Review*, *The New Yorker*, *Paris Review*, and other magazines. Her first collection of poems, *Ruin*, was published by Alice James Books and her second collection, *The Glimmering Room*, was published by Four Way Books in 2012. She has received fellowships from Yaddo and the MacDowell Colony as well as a Hodder Fellowship from Princeton University. She teaches at Sarah Lawrence College and lives in Brooklyn, New York.